Especially for

Grandma Irene

With warmest thoughts
and good wishes from

Pam Warneke

"Life is a beautiful garden,
An ever-growing thing,
But the blooms unfold with sharing
Whatever the day may bring."

A Garden
of Thoughts

Just for You

Selected by B. Fox
Illustrated by Sandra S. Arnold

Together in

We've been planted
in God's garden
where we're learning
still to grow,
There's so much
He wants to teach us,
so much we have to know.
It is certain we will blossom
with His tender love and care,
For he's placed us
beside others
that He knows
will help us there...

God's Garden

There's a special kind
of beauty
in the ones the Lord God chose,
And we know we have assurance
that He sees
how each one grows.
We've been planted
in God's garden
and we'll never be alone
For the Father
is the gardener
gently caring for His own.

Nature is
the living, visible
garment of God.

Goethe

Possibilities

If in a single flower we see
The wonder of life's mystery,
How beautiful
this world can be—
How filled with possibility!

Your life can be a garden
And a lovely place, indeed,
Where understanding is the soil,
Affection is the seed...

And if you tend each little plant
With love and hope and care,
Soon the flowers of happiness
Will bloom and flourish there.

He's
Always There

You'll find Him there
where trees and flowers grow.
You'll find Him there
where brooks and rivers flow.

You'll find Him there
where little children play.
You'll find Him there
where people kneel and pray.

You'll find Him there,
wherever you may be—
To hear your prayer,
to listen to your plea.

Spring comes but once a year
to cheer our way,
But He is always there—
day after day!

*H*is

*Every good and perfect gift
is from above...*

James 1:17

Precious Gifts

He has given us morning,
Brightness and sun,
Food to be eaten
And work to be done.

He has given us rainbows,
Flowers and song,
And the hand of a dear one
To help us along.

He has given us blessings
To brighten our way
And always - the gift
Of another new day.

A Quiet Pla

Keep a quiet little place
where only you can go,
A place securely set aside
to think,
to breathe, to grow...

...ce in the Heart

Don't think that you'll be
lonely there,
for God
is close beside you;
His messages
will all come through
to comfort and to guide you.
Life's burdens
grow much lighter
for all those who've set apart
A quiet place
for God to dwell
at peace within the heart.

The Heart of Friendship

Think of the sunshine
bursting through
an early morning haze.
Think of a carpet of violets
in springtime's golden days.

Picture the rocks that glisten
in a tiny bubbling brook.
Imagine the refreshment
of a shady little nook...

Think of fields of daisies
all abloom from end to end,

And among these things
that mean so much,
think of the heart of a friend.

In Celebration of Miracles

Miracles are
everywhere –
In sunlit fields
and sweet, clean air,
In flowers that bloom
and birds that sing –
There's wonder in
each living thing!

We are each of us a miracle,
unique in our own way,
For we all bring something lovely
of our own to every day.
And of all the people that I know,
there's no one else who brings
More joy to me than you—
or is so many special things.

You're
Very Special
to Me

*God knew from the beginning
just how special
you would be
And just how much
your thoughtful ways
would one day mean to me...*

He must have loved us
very much
to guide our steps
each day
And cared enough
to see to it
our paths would cross
this way.

$\mathcal{I}$'m thankful
every day I live
For the warmth
and kindness that you give,
Thankful
that in God's design,
He planned it so
your path crossed mine.

*G*od bless
and keep you
always.